What Nurse Practitioners Need to Know

Diane Lindsey Reeves

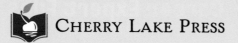

Published in the United States of America by Cherry Lake Publishing Group
Ann Arbor, Michigan
www.cherrylakepublishing.com

Reading Adviser: Beth Walker Gambro, MS, Ed., Reading Consultant, Yorkville, IL

Photo Credits: © PeopleImages.com - Yuri A/Shutterstock, cover, 1; Mathew Benjamin Brady, Public domain, via Wikimedia Commons, 5; © michaeljung/Shutterstock, 7; © Ground Picture/Shutterstock, 8; © Prostock-studio/Shutterstock, 9; © VGstockstudio/Shutterstock, 11; © ml_photo/Shutterstock, 12; © goodbishop/Shutterstock, 13; © Monkey Business Images/Shutterstock, 14; © New Africa/Shutterstock, 15; © wavebreakmedia/Shutterstock, 17; © LeventeGyori/Shutterstock, 18; © PeopleImages.com - Yuri A/Shutterstock, 21; © Pordee_Aomboon/Shutterstock, 22; © M-Production/Shutterstock, 23; © Monkey Business Image/Shutterstock, 25; © Gorodenkoff/Shutterstock, 26; © Inside Creative House/Shutterstock, 28; © CarlosDavid/Shutterstock, 29

Cherry Lake Press is an imprint of Cherry Lake Publishing Group.

Library of Congress Cataloging-in-Publication Data

Names: Reeves, Diane Lindsey, 1959- author.
Title: What nurse practitioners need to know / written by Diane Lindsey Reeves.
Description: Ann Arbor, Michigan : Cherry Lake Publishing, [2024] | Series: Career expert files | Audience: Grades 4-6 | Summary: "Nurse practitioners need to have the expert knowledge, skills, and tools to keep the world healthy. The Career Expert Files series covers professionals who are experts in their fields. These career experts know things we never thought they'd need to know, but we're glad they do"— Provided by publisher.
Identifiers: LCCN 2023035043 | ISBN 9781668939154 (paperback) | ISBN 9781668938119 (hardcover) | ISBN 9781668940495 (ebook) | ISBN 9781668941843 (pdf)
Subjects: LCSH: Nurse practitioners—Juvenile literature. | Nurse practitioners—Vocational guidance—Juvenile literature. | Nursing—Juvenile literature.
Classification: LCC RT82.8 .R44 2024 | DDC 610.7306/92—dc23/eng/20230828
LC record available at https://lccn.loc.gov/2023035043

Cherry Lake Publishing Group would like to acknowledge the work of the Partnership for 21st Century Learning, a Network of Battelle for Kids. Please visit Battelle for Kids online for more information.

Printed in the United States of America

Note from publisher: Websites change regularly, and their future contents are outside of our control. Supervise children when conducting any recommended online searches for extended learning opportunities.

Diane Lindsey Reeves likes to write books that help students figure out what they want to be when they grow up. She mostly lives in Washington, D.C., but spends as much time as she can in North Carolina and South Carolina with her grandkids.

CONTENTS

Introduction:

In the Know | 4

Chapter 1:

**Nurse Practitioners Know...
How to Make a Difference | 6**

Chapter 2:

**Nurse Practitioners Know...
How the Human Body Works | 10**

Chapter 3:

**Nurse Practitioners Know...
How to Use Medical Tools | 16**

Chapter 4:

**Nurse Practitioners Know...
How to Practice Medicine Safely | 20**

Chapter 5:

**Nurse Practitioners Know...
How to Find the Job They Want | 24**

Stop, Think, and Write | 30
Things to Do If You Want to Be a Nurse Practitioner | 30
Learn More | 31
Glossary, Index | 32

In the Know

Every career you can imagine has one thing in common. It takes an expert. Career experts need to know more about how to do a specific job than other people do. That is how everyone from plumbers to rocket scientists gets their job done.

Sometimes it takes years of college study to learn what they need to know. Other times, people learn by working alongside someone who is already a career expert. No matter how they learn, it takes a career expert to do any job well.

Take nurse practitioners (NPs), for instance. NPs want to help people get and stay well. They are healers. Training and experience prepare them to provide quality care.

What about you? Can you see yourself taking care of people in a hospital or doctor's office someday? Here are some things future nurse practitioners need to know.

Angel of the Battlefield

Clara Barton was a nurse who was famous for two things. She cared for soldiers during the Civil War (1861–1865). She also founded the American Red Cross. Barton helped locate more than 22,000 Union soldiers after the war. She got special permission from President Abraham Lincoln to help. She helped families find news about their loved ones. Barton was a self-taught nurse. There were no nursing schools at that time.

CHAPTER 1

Nurse Practitioners Know...How to Make a Difference

Some people talk about making the world a better place. Nurse practitioners actually do it. They work in the places sick people come for care. These include a doctor's office, a school, or an urgent care clinic. Some work in hospitals or even prisons. They come to work every day to help people.

NPs play an important role in health care. They are qualified to do more than a nurse. But they can't do as much as a doctor. They assess problems and **diagnose** diseases. They order medical tests and prescribe medications. Sometimes they help doctors figure out challenging cases.

Nurse practitioners spend time developing personal relationships with their patients in order to better understand how to properly and fully care for their needs.

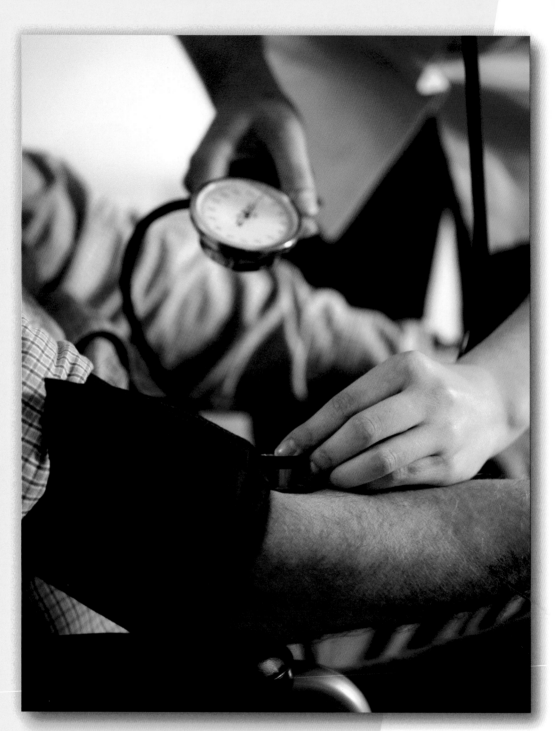

NPs take their patients' vitals, including height, weight, blood pressure, and temperature.

In the United States, over a billion people see NPs every year. Sometimes there are not enough doctors to go around. This is especially true in rural communities. There is a doctor shortage. One reason is that more people are living longer. As people get older, they need more health care.

Nurse practitioners fill the gap. They help make health care more available. There are benefits to seeing an NP. One is that NPs often spend more time with patients. That gives them a chance to get to know patients. It allows them to talk with them about health concerns.

NP VERSUS PA

Nurse practitioners and **physician's assistants** (PAs) are similar. The big difference is that NPs are registered nurses first. They already have health care experience. PAs may or may not have health care experience before starting a PA program. NPs are more specialized in the type of care they provide. PAs are more general.

CHAPTER 2

Nurse Practitioners Know...How the Human Body Works

Why do you have to learn about science in school? If you ever want to be an NP, pay extra attention. NPs must not only know a lot about biology. And they don't just need to know chemistry and anatomy. They must also put that knowledge to work every day.

Biology is life science. It helps NPs understand how family history affects patient health. Chemistry is a physical science. Chemistry helps nurses understand how diseases affect the body. It also helps them understand how medicines work.

Recording a patient's family history is important. It helps NPs determine biological risks for their patients.

Pharmacology uses both biology and chemistry. NPs use it to decide which and how much medicine to prescribe. Without biology and chemistry, NPs could make mistakes. These mistakes might harm a patient.

Body structures and systems are covered in anatomy. Nurses know where each organ is located. They know what each is supposed to do. That way, they know when something is wrong.

NPs also learn how to treat patients. They know how to stitch up wounds. They know how to set fractured bones. They are skilled in giving shots and drawing blood. They learn how to order tests. They learn how to analyze results.

NPs must become disease detectives. They look for clues as they examine patients. Those clues help them diagnose problems.

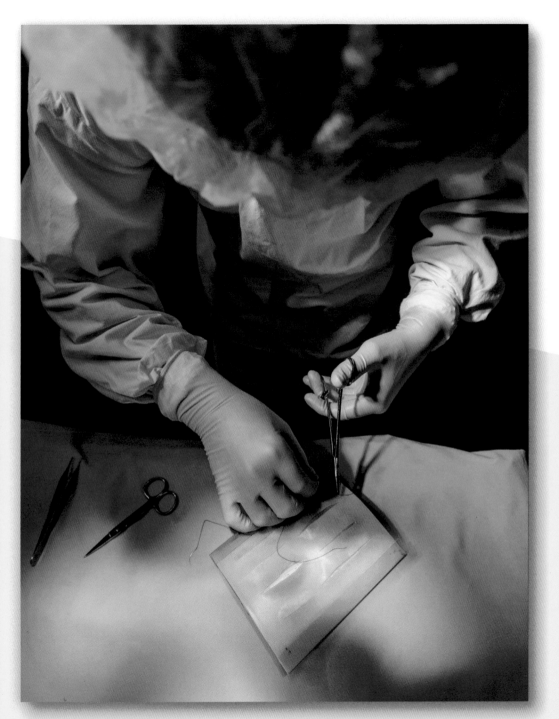

NPs spend many hundreds of hours practicing stitches and other procedures so they can perform them correctly on patients when the time comes.

Helping patients recover can involve a whole care team that might include doctors, nurse practitioners, surgeons, physical therapists, and more!

Good NPs have a pleasant **bedside manner**. They are kind and listen to what patients say. They help patients relax. Patients may then share details about how they feel. This helps the NP figure out what patients need.

There's one more thing NPs need to know. They need to know when to ask for help. Sometimes they need someone else to examine a patient's symptoms. NPs team up with doctors and other health professionals. This gives patients the best care possible.

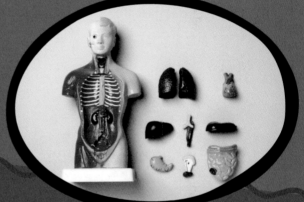

WHAT GOES WHERE

Get a big piece of paper. Draw the outline of a human body on it. Use books and online resources to find information. Research how the human body works. Use markers to show where different organs are located. Start with the heart, lungs, and brain. Then locate the organs that fill a person's **torso**. These include the bladder, kidney, large intestine, liver, and pancreas. Be sure to include the stomach, spleen, and small intestine. Also, try to describe what each organ does!

CHAPTER 3

Nurse Practitioners Know...How to Use Medical Tools

Maybe you have noticed some of the tools NPs use. They start the exam by checking your weight and height. They use thermometers to check your body temperature. They may click a pulse oximeter on your finger. This measures your blood's oxygen level. It tells how well oxygen is binding to your red blood cells.

Sometimes they attach a cuff to your upper arm. Then they pump it full of air. As it tightens around your arm, it measures your heart rate. This device is a blood pressure cuff.

An NP may take your temperature to check for a fever. A fever can be a clear sign

A shortcut to finding a pulse is to count the number of heartbeats in 15 seconds and multiply by 4.

NPs don't need a medical device to feel your pulse. They put two fingers on your neck or wrist. They count how many times your heart beats in 1 minute. That tells them how well blood is flowing in your body.

You can probably recognize the stethoscope they carry. They wear it around their necks. They use this to listen

They are likely to use a penlight. This helps them get a good look at your eyes. They can use it to look in your mouth. They can use it to look at your throat. They peek into your ears with an otoscope. It lets them see your ear canal and eardrums.

NPs use a smartphone or smart device to record patient information. They record all the details of your exam. They also use these devices to order **prescriptions**. They use them to schedule tests.

Sometimes a basic exam reveals a problem. Then NPs may order additional tests. These tests can include x-rays or ultrasound exams. Ultrasound exams help look inside a patient's body. They may also include blood tests. Someone's blood reveals all kinds of clues about their health.

THUMP, THUMP, THUMP

You can check your own or another person's pulse. Take the first two fingers of your right hand. Place them on your left hand, under your thumb. Press down gently until you feel a beat. Count the beats for 15 seconds. Then multiply the number of beats times four. That is your heart rate. A normal heart rate for kids ranges from 75 to 118 beats per minute (bpm). To watch an online video, ask an adult to help you search for "how to take your pulse."

CHAPTER 4

Nurse Practitioners Know...How to Practice Medicine Safely

Nurse practitioners often face life-or-death situations when treating patients. Patients count on them to make careful decisions. They expect them to help and not harm.

Medicine is a big area where NPs must be careful. They must be absolutely certain to prescribe the correct medicine. They need to be certain they prescribe the correct **dosage**. They consider any allergies a patient has. They ensure a patient's medications work well together. Even misspelling the name of a medicine can be dangerous. This is where checking—and double-checking—your work is a must.

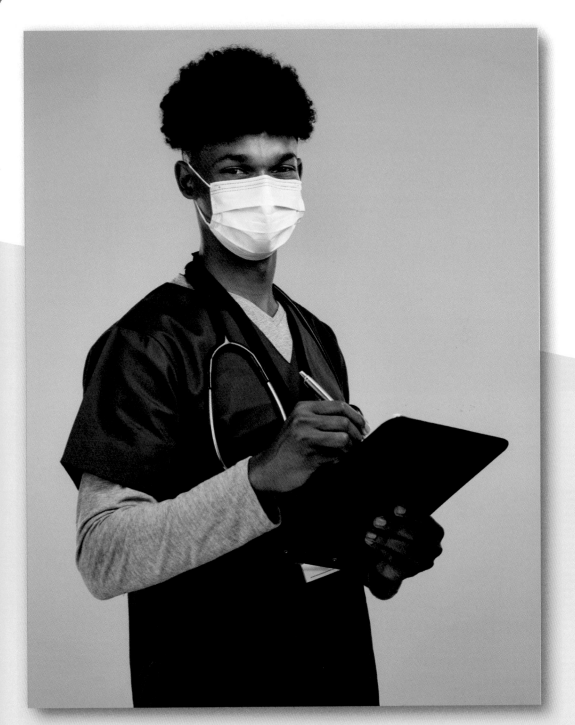

NPs and doctors use charts to keep track of a patients' medical history and needs so they can be sure they are providing the best care.

During the COVID-19 pandemic, all people who worked in medical settings took special care to mask up and use other personal protective equipment.

The COVID pandemic reminded everyone to beware of germs. This is especially true in medical care. NPs make sure to mask up and scrub up. This helps to prevent spreading germs. They disinfect surfaces used by patients. Using **sterile** needles and instruments keeps patients safe.

NPs practice safe medicine. They do this by looking at the bigger picture. They don't just consider one set of symptoms. They take a **holistic** approach. That means they consider the whole patient. This includes how physical, mental, emotional, and social factors affect them.

Nurse practitioners also play a big role in patient education. They explain the benefits of healthy choices. They make sure that patients understand how to use medications. Their job is to improve patient outcomes by encouraging healthy habits.

PERSONAL 911

Accidents happen and people get sick. Sometimes you can help yourself and others before seeing an NP. Use index cards to write down tips. These can be tips for dealing with minor medical emergencies. Use books or online information to gather knowledge. Search for how to handle common first aid problems. What do you do if you get a bee sting? What if you burn or cut yourself? How do you clean a minor wound? What should you do if you sprain your ankle? How do you remove a splinter? Basic first aid can be helpful. You can feel more comfortable. Then you can see a health professional.

CHAPTER 5

Nurse Practitioners Know...How to Find the Job They Want

Nurse practitioners must make two big decisions during their training. One is the environment they want to work in. Do they want to work in a hospital setting? Or would they prefer to work in a doctor's office?

The second decision is what population they want to serve. Do they want to work with adults or children? Do they want to focus on one health care problem? This decision guides the classes they take. It also sets them on the best career path.

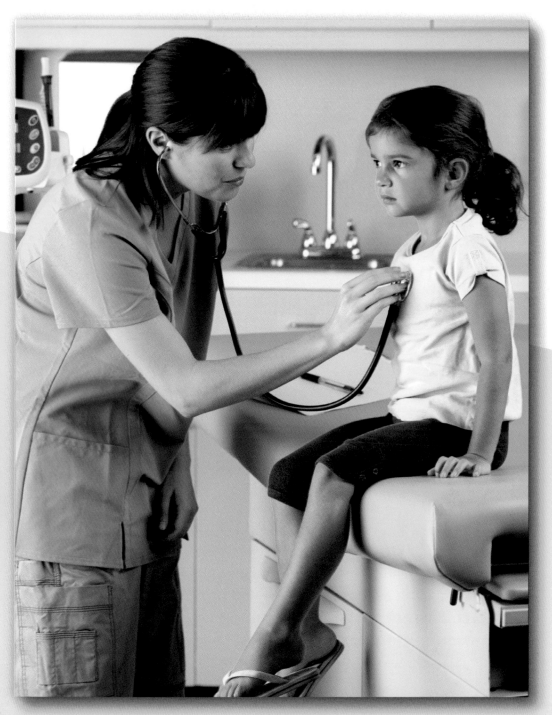

When NPs work with kids, they are working in pediatrics, which is the branch of medicine that specifically deals with caring for children.

Almost 70 percent of nurse practitioners are primary care NPs. This means they are qualified to provide general care. They can provide this for patients of all ages. They can provide this for patients of all backgrounds. Millions of people choose NPs to provide their everyday health care. NPs see patients for **acute illnesses** like colds and the flu. They also treat patients with **chronic illnesses**. These patients require ongoing care over time.

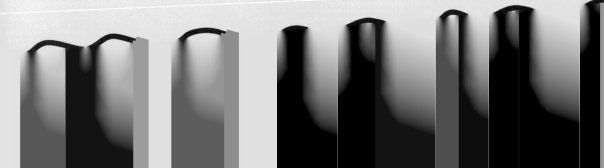

TRUE OR FALSE

A nurse practitioner can do everything that a doctor can.

Answer: False. Nurse practitioners can do many things that doctors do, such as treat illnesses and prescribe medicines. However, they are not allowed to perform surgery. They also need a doctor's help to deliver babies.

Over 350,000 babies are born a day to mothers all over the world. Nurse practitioners help make sure mom and baby stay safe and healthy during the delivery process.

Other NPs prefer to work with more specific populations. For instance, they might work only with adults. They might work only with the elderly. Elder care is called geriatrics.

Neonatal NPs take care of premature and sick newborns. They often work in hospital neonatal intensive care units

Doctors and nurse practitioners who provide care solely focused on people 65 and over are in the field of geriatrics.

You have to be an expert to be a nurse practitioner. You have to work and study hard!

Pediatric NPs care for babies, toddlers, children, and young adults. They can choose to provide primary or acute care.

Some NPs focus on mental health care. They work with patients with psychiatric disorders.

Other NPs choose to work only with women. Sometimes they provide general health care. They may work with pregnant women and help deliver babies.

Nurse practitioners play an important role in health care. They make expert health care available to more people.

Activity

Stop, Think, and Write

Nurse practitioners take care of people when they are sick. Can you imagine a world without nurse practitioners?

Get a separate sheet of paper. On one side, answer these questions:

- *How do nurse practitioners make the world a better place?*
- *If you were a nurse practitioner, what kind would you want to be?*
- *Where would you want to work?*

On the other side of the paper:

- *Draw a picture of you taking good care of a patient.*

Things to Do If You Want to Be a Nurse Practitioner

NOW

- Take a first aid or **cardiopulmonary resuscitation** (CPR) class through the Red Cross or your local community center.
- Ask a parent or teacher to help arrange for you to job shadow a nurse practitioner.
- Take lots of science and math classes in school and study to get good grades.

LATER

- Check to see if your local high school offers a health sciences career academy.
- Become a registered nurse by first earning a college degree in nursing.
- Get experience working in a clinical setting in a hospital or doctor's office.
- Complete a master's level nurse practitioner degree.
- Pass the nurse practitioner certification exam.

Learn More

Books

Gobin, Shantel. *Careers to Help Others.* Vero Beach, FL: Rourke Books, 2023.

Jazynka, Kiston. *Florence Nightingale.* New York, NY: DK Publishing, 2019.

MacDonald, Fiona. *You Wouldn't Want to Live Without Nurses.* New York, NY: Scholastic, 2017.

Rhatigan, Joe. *Get a Job at the Hospital.* Ann Arbor, MI: Cherry Lake, 2017.

On the Web

With an adult, learn more online with these suggested searches.

Explore Health Careers

How the Human Body Works

Johnson and Johnson Real Nurses, Real Stories

What Is a Nurse Practitioner?

Glossary

acute illnesses (uh-KYOOT IL-nuhs-ez) sicknesses that occur very quickly and last a short time

bedside manner (BED-siyd MAN-uhr) behavior toward patients to help them feel comfortable

cardiopulmonary resuscitation (kahr-dee-oh-PUL-muh-nair-ee ri-suh-suh-TAY-shuhn) also called CPR; an emergency lifesaving procedure used when someone's heart stops beating

chronic illnesses (KRAH-nik IL-nuhs-ez) health conditions that last one year or more and require ongoing medical attention, such as heart disease, cancer, and diabetes

diagnose (DIYE-ig-nohs) examine a patient's symptoms to figure out what is causing an illness

dosage (DOH-sij) the amount of a medicine or drug that a patient should take and how often they need to take it

holistic (hoh-LIH-stik) medical treatment that involves the patient's entire body, including their mind

physician's assistants (fuh-ZIH-shuhnz uh-SIH-stuhnts) health care workers who examine, diagnose, and treat patients under a doctor's supervision

prescriptions (prih-SKRIP-shuhnz) written instructions for the preparation and use of a medicine; patients take prescriptions to drug stores to be filled

sterile (STAIR-uhl) totally clean and free from living organisms and microorganisms

torso (TOR-soh) the main part of the human body, not including the head, arms, and legs

Index

activities, 15, 19, 23, 30
American Red Cross, 5
anatomy, 12, 15

Barton, Clara, 5
bedside manner, 15
biology, 10, 12

careers and jobs, 24–30
chemistry, 10, 12
COVID-19, 22

diagnoses, 6, 12
doctors, 6, 9, 26

education and training, 5, 10, 12–13, 24, 30
expertise, 4

first aid, 23

geriatrics, 27–28

health care systems, 9, 14, 29
human body, 10, 12, 15

medical safety, 20–23
medical tests, 19

nurse practitioners
  careers, 24–30
  skills and talents, 4, 10–15, 30
  work roles and methods, 6–9, 16–23, 26–29

organs, 12, 15

patient care, 6–12, 14–23, 26–29
patient populations, 24–29
pediatrics, 25, 27, 29
pharmacology, 12
physician assistants (PAs), 9
prescriptions, 6, 12, 19–20
pulse-taking, 18–19

safety, 20–23
science education, 10, 12, 30
stitches, 13

tools, 16–19, 21

U.S. Civil War, 5